ESSENTIAL HOME LIBRARY S

VOLUME 7: 1990–200

Songs That Define an Era

Alfred Publishing Co., Inc.
16320 Roscoe Blvd., Suite 100
P.O. Box 10003
Van Nuys, CA 91410-0003
alfred.com

ISBN-10: 0-7390-4217-3
ISBN-13: 978-0-7390-4217-5

Contents

Song	Artist	Page
ALL I WANNA DO	SHERYL CROW	8
AMAZED	LONESTAR	16
ANGEL EYES	JIM BRICKMAN	3
BECAUSE YOU LOVED ME	CELINE DION	20
BELIEVE	CHER	25
BREAKFAST AT TIFFANY'S	DEEP BLUE SOMETHING	30
COMING OUT OF THE DARK	GLORIA ESTEFAN	35
COULD I HAVE THIS KISS FOREVER	WHITNEY HOUSTON & ENRIQUE IGLESIAS	40
DREAMING OF YOU	SELENA	46
GRADUATION (FRIENDS FOREVER)	VITAMIN C	52
HERO	MARIAH CAREY	66
HOW DO I LIVE	LEANN RIMES	70
I DON'T WANT TO MISS A THING	AEROSMITH	59
I SWEAR	ALL-4-ONE	74
I'LL BE THERE FOR YOU	THE REMBRANDTS	78
I'LL NEVER GET OVER YOU GETTING OVER ME	EXPOSÉ	84
LOSING MY RELIGION	R.E.M.	90
LOVE WILL KEEP US ALIVE	EAGLES	96
MACARENA	LOS DEL RÍO	106
MUSIC OF MY HEART	GLORIA ESTEFAN & ★NSYNC	112
NOW AND FOREVER	RICHARD MARX	118
SMOOTH	SANTANA FEATURING ROB THOMAS	101
THIS KISS	FAITH HILL	122
UN-BREAK MY HEART	TONI BRAXTON	140
VALENTINE	JIM BRICKMAN	126
VOGUE	MADONNA	132

ANGEL EYES

Composed by
JIM BRICKMAN

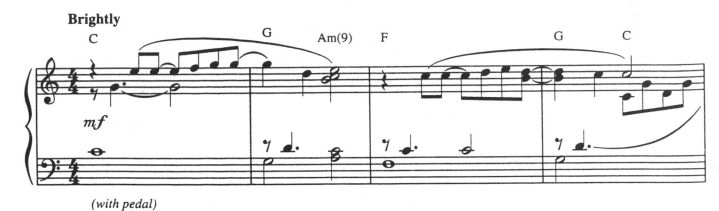

(with pedal)

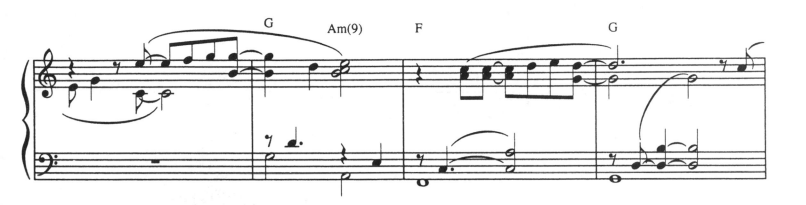

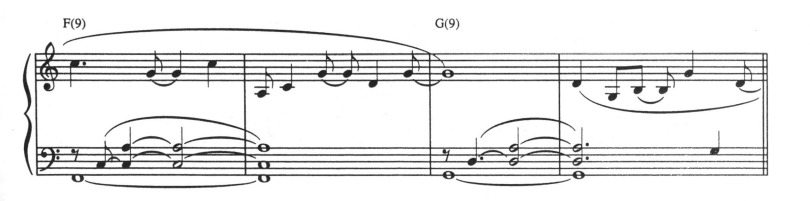

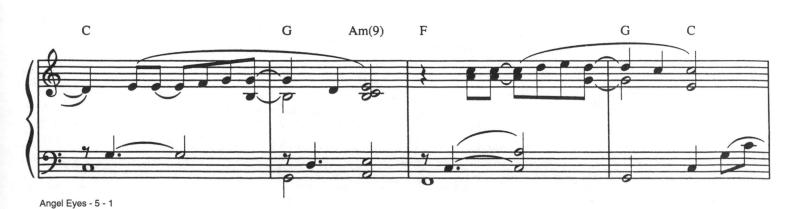

Angel Eyes - 5 - 1

4

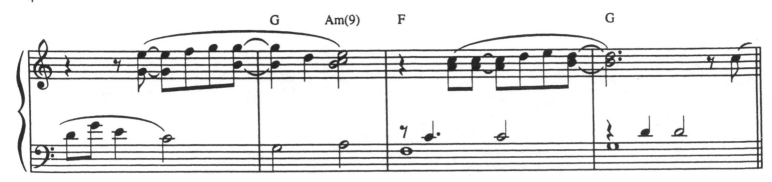

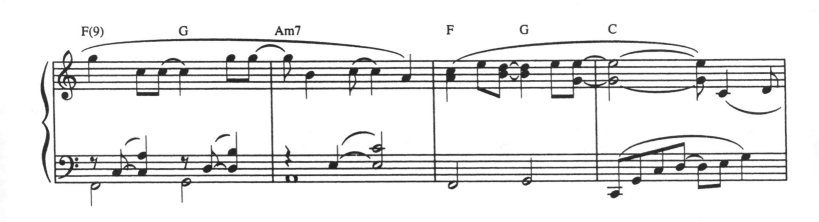

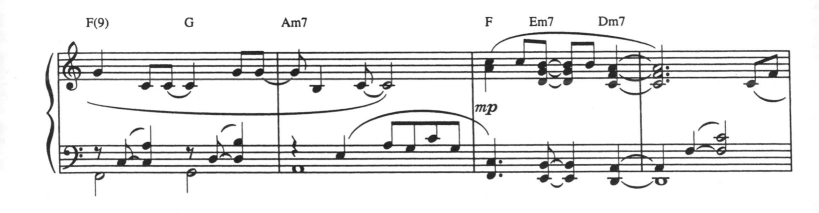

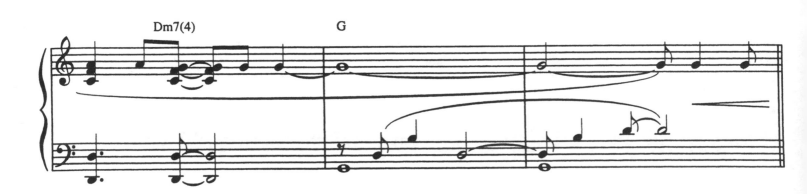

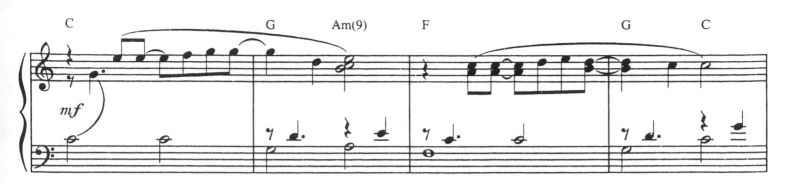

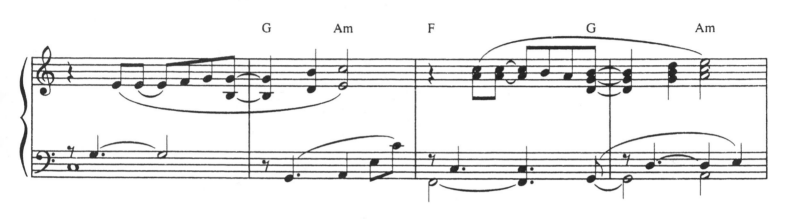

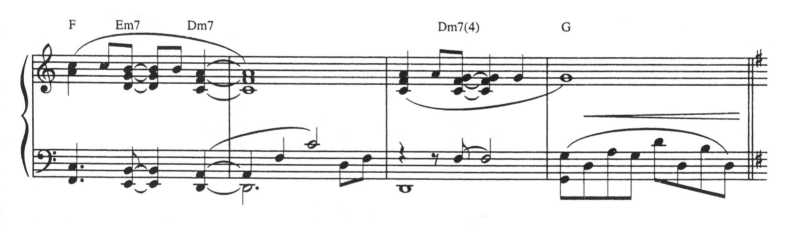

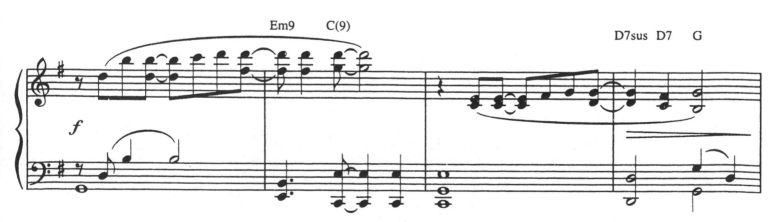

6

ALL I WANNA DO

Words and Music by
SHERYL CROW, WYN COOPER, KEVIN GILBERT,
BILL BOTTRELL and DAVID BAERWALD

12

⊕ *Coda*

C7 D9

I've got a feel - ing the par - ty has just___ be - gun. All I wan-na

E7 C7

do is have some fun,___ I won't tell___ you that you're the on -

D9 E7

- ly one. All I wan - na do is have some fun,___ un - til the

C7 D9 E7

sun comes up o - ver San - ta Mon - i - ca Boul - e - vard,___

Verse 3:
I like a good beer buzz early in the morning,
And Billy likes to peel the labels from his bottles of Bud
And shred them on the bar.
Then he lights every match in an oversized pack,
Letting each one burn down to his thick fingers
Before blowing and cursing them out.
And he's watching the Buds as they spin on the floor.
A happy couple enters the bar dancing dangerously close to one another.
The bartender looks up from his want ads.
(To Chorus:)

AMAZED

Words and Music by
MARV GREEN, AIMEE MAYO
and CHRIS LINDSEY

Amazed - 4 - 1

Verse 2:
The smell of your skin,
The taste of your kiss,
The way you whisper in the dark.
Your hair all around me,
Baby, you surround me;
You touch every place in my heart.
Oh, it feels like the first time every time.
I wanna spend the whole night in your eyes.
(To Chorus:)

BECAUSE YOU LOVED ME
(Theme from *Up Close & Personal*)

Words and Music by
DIANE WARREN

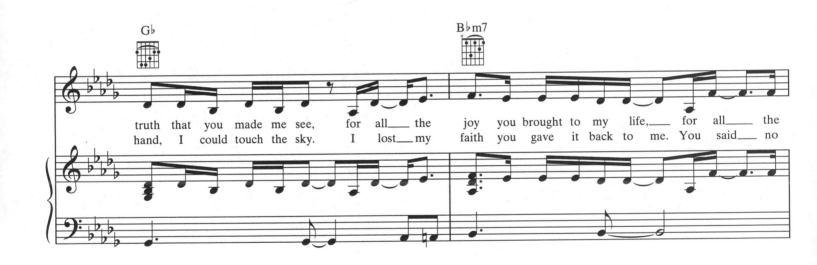

BELIEVE

Words and Music by
BRIAN HIGGINS, STUART McLENNAN,
PAUL BARRY, STEPHEN TORCH,
MATT GRAY and TIM POWELL

Moderate disco beat ♩ = 132

Verse:

1. No mat-ter how hard I try you keep push-ing
2. What am I sup-posed to do, sit a-round and

me a-side and I can't break through, there's no
wait for you, and I can't do that, there's no

* Original recording in G♭ major.

Believe - 5 - 1

Chorus:

Do you be - lieve___ in life___ af - ter love?___ I can feel___ some-thing in - side___ me say,___ I real-ly don't think you're strong___ e - nough, no.___

Do you be - lieve___ in life___ af - ter love?___ I can feel ___ some-thing in - side___ me say,___ I real-ly don't think you're strong___ e - nough, no.___

Repeat ad lib. and fade

BREAKFAST AT TIFFANY'S

Words and Music by
TODD PIPES

Moderately ♩ = 104

Verse:

see you,___ the on-ly one___ who knew___ me, but
3. You'll say___ we got noth-ing in com-mon, no
the we got noth-ing in com-mon, no

31

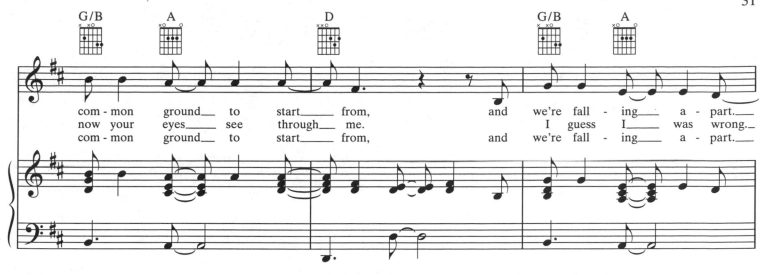

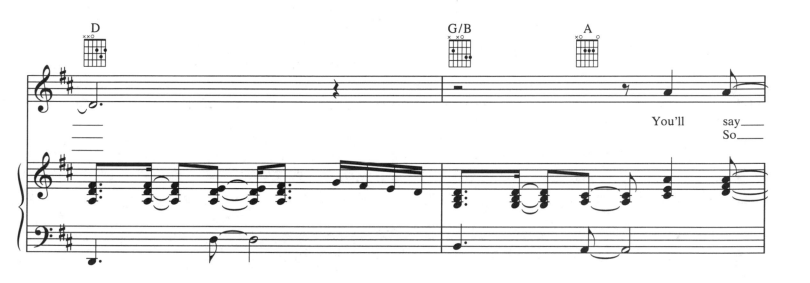

Breakfast at Tiffany's - 5 - 2

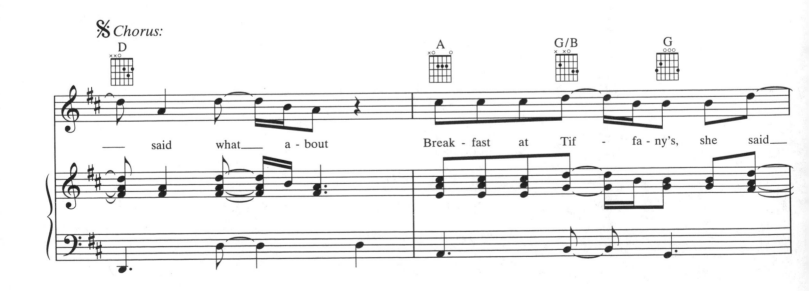

COMING OUT OF THE DARK

Words and Music by
GLORIA ESTEFAN, EMILIO ESTEFAN, JR.
and JON SECADA

1. Why be a - fraid _____ if I'm not a - lone? _____ Life is nev - er
2. Start - ing a - gain _____ is part of _ the _ plan, _____ and I'll be so much

eas - y, _____ the rest is _ un - known. _____ And up till now for
strong - er _____ hold - ing _ your _ hand. _____ Step by step I'll

Coming Out of the Dark - 5 - 1

COULD I HAVE THIS KISS FOREVER

Words and Music by
DIANE WARREN

Verse:

1. O - ver___ and o - ver,___ I look in___ your eyes. You are
2. O - ver___ and o - ver,___ I've dreamed of___ this night. Now you're

Could I Have This Kiss Forever - 6 - 1

DREAMING OF YOU

Words and Music by
TOM SNOW and
FRANNE GOLDE

Moderately ♩ = 88

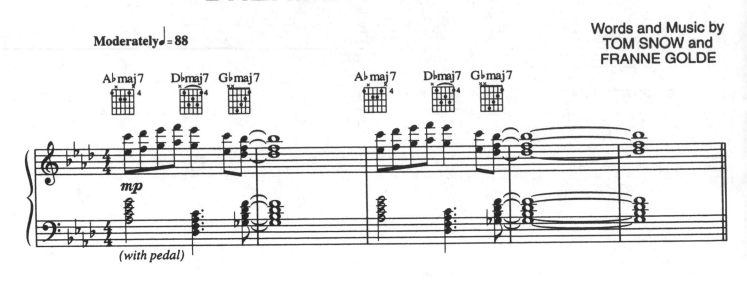

(with pedal)

Verse:

1. Late at night when all the world___ is sleep-ing, I stay up and think of you.___ And I

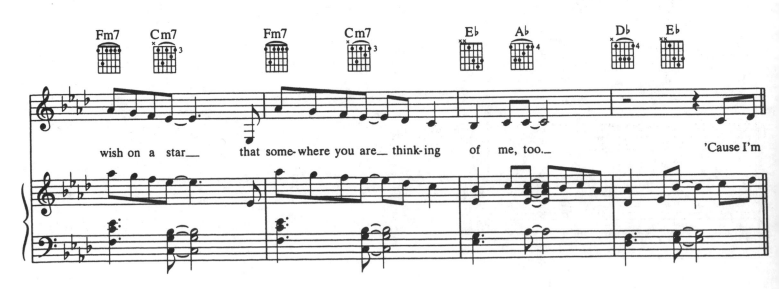

wish on a star___ that some-where you are___ think-ing of me, too.___ 'Cause I'm

Chorus:

dream - ing___ of you to - night.___ Till to - mor - row,___ I'll be

hold - ing you tight.___ And there's no - where in___ the world I'd rath - er be than

here in my room,___ dream - ing a - bout___ you and me._____

48

2. Won-der if you ev-er see____ me and I won-der if you know I'm there.____
3. I just wan-na hold you close____ but so far, all I have are dreams of you.____

If you looked in my eyes,____ would you see what's in-side?__ Would you
So, I wait for the day____ and the cour-age to say__ how much

e - ven care?_____
I love you._____

Yes, I do. I'll be

50

Dreaming of You - 6 - 5

GRADUATION
(Friends Forever)

Words and Music by
COLLEEN FITZPATRICK
and JOSH DEUTSCH

Graduation - 7 - 1

friends for - ev - er.

friends for - ev - er.

rit.

Verse 2:
So if we get the big jobs and we make the big money,
When we look back at now, will our jokes still be funny?
Will we still remember everything we learned in school,
Still be trying to break every single rule?
Will little brainy Bobby be the stockbroker man?
Can Heather find a job that won't interfere with her tan?
I keep, keep thinking that it's not goodbye,
Keep on thinking it's our time to fly.
And this is how it feels…
(To Chorus:)

Verse 3:
Will we think about tomorrow like we think about now?
Can we survive it out there, can we make it somehow?
I guess I thought that this would never end,
And suddenly it's like we're women and men.
Will the past be a shadow that will follow us around?
Will the memories fade when I leave this town?
I keep, keep thinking that it's not goodbye,
Keep thinking it's our time to fly.
(To Chorus:)

From Touchstone Pictures' ARMAGEDDON

I DON'T WANT TO MISS A THING

Words and Music by
DIANE WARREN

60

HERO

By
WALTER AFANASIEFF and MARIAH CAREY

Moderate ballad

Hero - 4 - 1

From the Touchstone Motion Picture "CON AIR"

HOW DO I LIVE

Words and Music by
DIANE WARREN

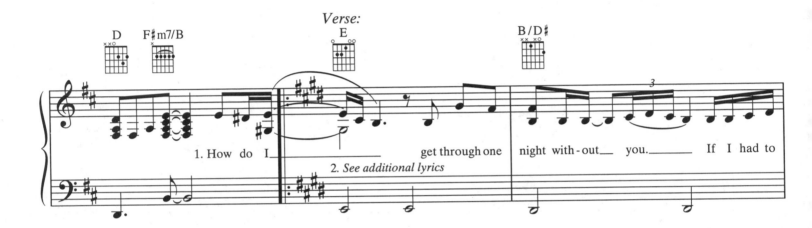

How Do I Live - 4 - 1

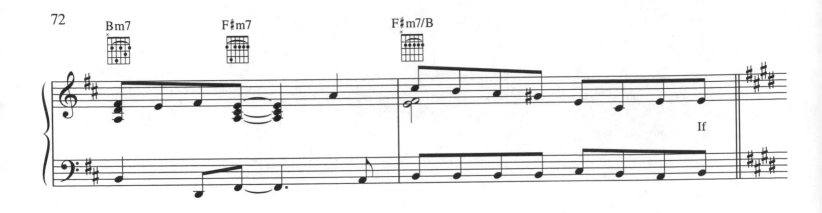

Bm7   F#m7   F#m7/B

If

Bridge:

G#m7   C#m7   F#m7

you ev - er leave,_____ ba - by, you would take a - way___ ev - 'ry - thing.___

G#m7   C#m7   F#m7

Need you with me._____ Ba - by, 'coz you know that you're ev - 'ry - thing___

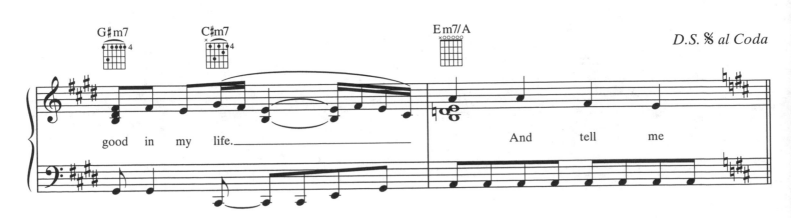

G#m7   C#m7   Em7/A   *D.S. % al Coda*

good in my life._____ And tell me

Coda

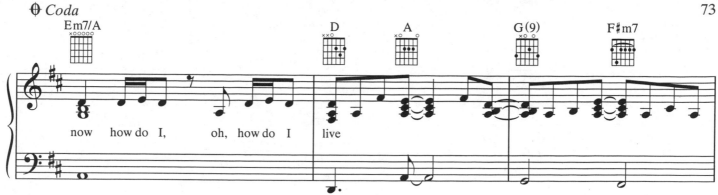

now how do I, oh, how do I live

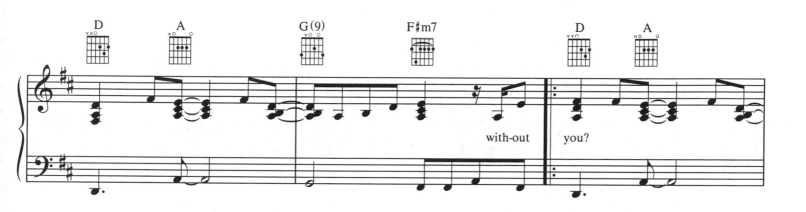

with-out you?

Repeat ad lib. and fade
(vocal 1st time only)

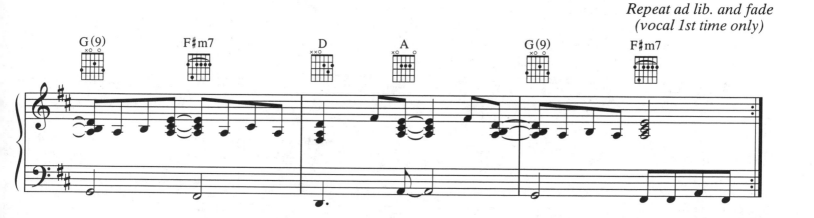

Verse 2:
Without you, there'd be no sun in my sky,
There would be no love in my life,
There'd be no world left for me.
And I, baby, I don't know what I would do,
I'd be lost if I lost you.
If you ever leave,
Baby, you would take away everything real in my life.
And tell me now...
(To Chorus:)

I SWEAR

Words and Music by
GARY BAKER and FRANK MYERS

I'LL BE THERE FOR YOU
(Theme from "Friends")

Words by
DAVID CRANE, MARTA KAUFFMAN, ALLEE WILLIS,
PHIL SOLEM and DANNY WILDE

Music by
MICHAEL SKLOFF

I'll Be There for You - 6 - 1

I'll Be There for You - 6 - 2

* Guitar fill reads 8va.

I'll Be There for You - 6 - 3

I'LL NEVER GET OVER
YOU GETTING OVER ME

Words and Music by
DIANE WARREN

I'll Never Get Over You Getting Over Me - 6 - 1

I'll Never Get Over You Getting Over Me - 6 - 4

LOSING MY RELIGION

Words and Music by
WILLIAM BERRY, PETER BUCK,
MIKE MILLS and MICHAEL STIPE

92

Losing My Religion - 6 - 3

LOVE WILL KEEP US ALIVE

Words and Music by
JIM CAPALDI, PETER VALE
and PAUL CARRACK

Moderately slow ♩ = 88

Verses 1 - 3:

stand - ing,___ all a - lone___ a - gainst the world out - side.___
wor - ry,___ some - times you've just___ got to let it ride.___
found___ you,___ there's no more emp - ti - ness in - side.___

1.4. I was

Love Will Keep Us Alive - 5 - 1

SMOOTH

Music and Lyrics by
ITAAL SHUR and ROB THOMAS

Moderately ♩ = 114

Smooth - 5 - 1

same as the e-mo-tion that I get from you.____ You got the kind of lov-ing that can

be so smooth,__ yeah.

To Coda 1.

Give me your heart,__ make it real____ or else for-get a-bout it.

D.S. 𝄋 *al Coda*

2.

2. Well, I'll tell you ____ or else for-get a-bout it.

Smooth - 5 - 4

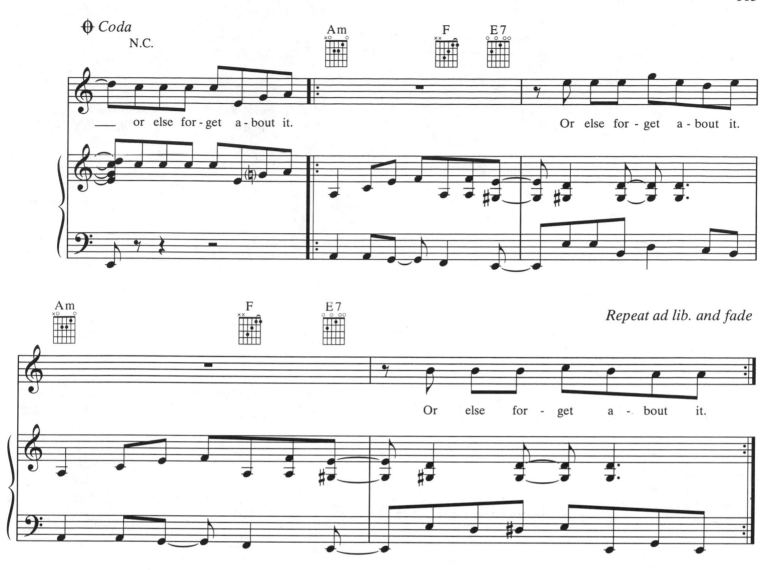

Verse 2:
Well, I'll tell you one thing,
If you would leave, it be a crying shame.
In every breath and every word
I hear your name calling me out, yeah.
Well, out from the barrio,
You hear my rhythm on your radio.
You feel the tugging of the world,
So soft and slow, turning you 'round and 'round.
(To Pre-Chorus:)

MACARENA

Words and Music by
ANTONIO ROMERO and RAFAEL RUIZ

Da - le_a tu cuer - po_a-le-grí - a Ma-ca - re - na que tu cuer-po_es pa' dar - le_a-le-grí-a y co-sa bue-na.

Macarena - 6 - 1

Da - le a tu cuer - po a - le - grí - a Ma - ca - re - na, eh,_____ Ma - ca - re - na.

Da - le a tu cuer - po a - le - grí - a Ma - ca - re - na que tu cuer - po es pa' dar - le a - le - grí - a y co - sa bue - na.

Da - le a tu cuer - po a - le - grí - a Ma - ca - re - na, eh,_____ Ma - ca - re - na. 1. Ma - ca -

Versos 1 y 3:

re - na tie - ne un no - vio que se lla - ma, que se lla - ma de a - pe - lli - do Vi - to - ri - no. Y en la
3. *See additional lyric*

Da - le a tu cuer - po a-le-grí - a Ma-ca - re - na, eh,_____ Ma - ca - re - na.

Da - le a tu cuer - po a-le - grí - a Ma-ca - re - na que tu cuer-po es pa' dar - le a-le-grí - a y co - sa bue-na.

Da - le a tu cuer - po a-le - grí - a Ma-ca - re - na, eh,_____ Ma - ca - re - na. 2. Ma-ca-

Versos 2 y 4:

re - na, Ma-ca - re - na, Ma-ca - re - na, que te gus-tan los ve - ra-nos de Mar-be - lla. Ma-ca-
4. *See additional lyric*

Da - le a tu cuer - po a - le - grí - a Ma - ca - re - na, eh,_____ Ma - ca - re - na.

Verso 3:
Macarena sueña con el Corte inglés
Y se compra los modelos mas modernos.
Le gustaría vivir en Nueva York
Y ligar un novio nuevo.

Puente 2:
Macarena sueña con el Corte inglés
Y se compra los modelos mas modernos.
Le gustaría vivir en Nueva York
Y ligar un novio nuevo.
(Al Coro:)

Verso 4:
Macarena tiene un novio que se llama,
Que se llama de apellido Vitorino.
Y en la jura de bandera del muchacho
Se la dió con dos amigos.

Puente 3:
Macarena tiene un novio que se llama,
Que se llama de apellido Vitorino.
Y en la jura de bandera del muchacho
Se la dió con dos amigos.
(Al Coro:)

From the Miramax Motion Picture "Music Of The Heart"

MUSIC OF MY HEART

Words and Music by
DIANE WARREN

NOW AND FOREVER

Words and Music by
RICHARD MARX

If I'd on-ly known__ you were there__ all the time,__ all this time.__

Un-til the day__ the o-cean does-n't touch__ the sand,__

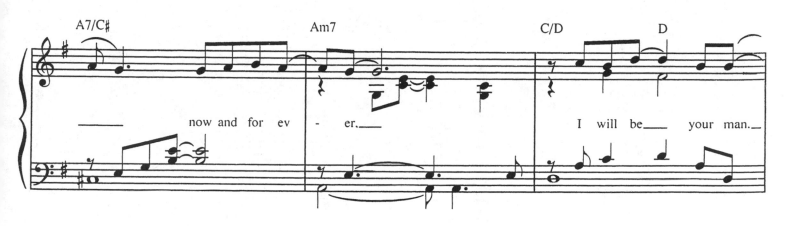

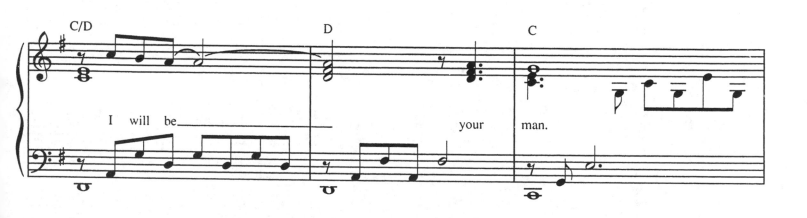

THIS KISS

Words and Music by
ROBIN LERNER, ANNIE ROBOFF
and BETH NIELSEN CHAPMAN

Moderately, with double-time feel ♩ = 64

1. I don't want an-oth-er heart-break. I don't need an-oth-er turn to cry,_____ no.
2. Cin-der-el-la said to Snow White, "How does love get so off course?"_____ Oh.

I don't want to learn the hard way. Ba-by,
All I want-ed was a white knight with a

hel-lo, oh no, good-bye.
good heart, soft touch, fast horse.

This Kiss - 4 - 1

Chorus:

VALENTINE

Composed by
JIM BRICKMAN and
JACK KUGELL

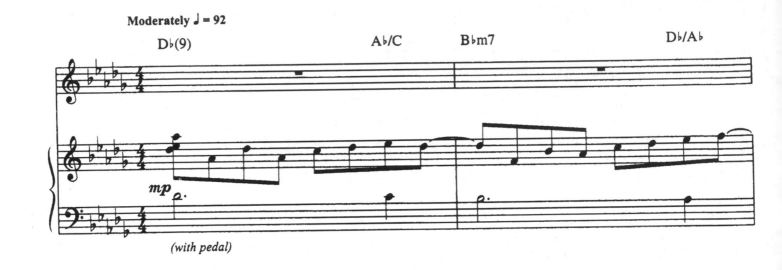

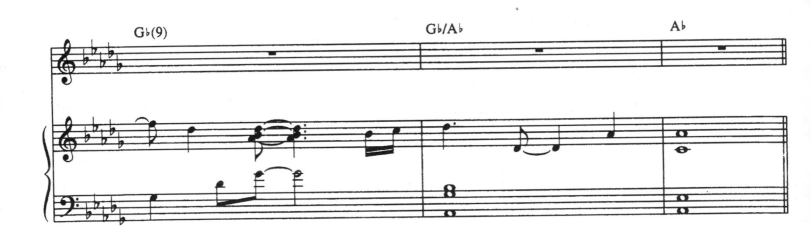

If there were no words,_____ no way to speak,_____ I

Valentine - 6 - 1

VOGUE

Words and Music by
MADONNA CICCONE and SHEP PETTIBONE

Vogue - 8 - 1

Vogue,

Vogue, *Vogue.*

Ab
4fr.
No chord

Look a - round, ev - 'ry - where you turn is heart - ache, it's ev - 'ry - where that you go. _____
All you need is your own im - ag - i - na - tion, so use it, that's what it's for. _____

_____ You try ev - 'ry - thing you can to es - cape
_____ Go in - side, for your fin - est in - spir - a - tion;

UN-BREAK MY HEART

Words and Music by
DIANE WARREN

Verse:

1. Don't leave me in___ all this pain,___ don't leave me out__ in the rain.___
2. Take back that sad__ word good - bye,___ bring back the joy__ to my life._____

Un-Break My Heart - 5 - 1